Filled Marriage

VIDEO STUDY

Dr. Tim & Darcy Kimmel

Name:_____

family matters

building grace-based relationships

Scottsdale, Arizona
1-800-467-4596
familymatters.net

Grace Filled Marriage Video Study

This workbook is to be used in conjunction with the *Grace Filled Marriage Video Study* and is not meant to be a stand-alone piece.

Requests for information should be addressed to:

Family Matters®
P.O. Box 14382
Scottsdale, AZ 85267-4382
familymatters.net
800-467-4596

Published by Family Matters®

Cover design by The Black Rhinos (www.theblackrhinos.com)

Printed in the United States of America

v2.18.15

Contents

Welcome!

Thanks for caring enough to take time out of your busy lives to learn how to have a grace-filled marriage.

If you've been married for any length of time, you already know, that while marriage can be the best thing that ever happened to you, it can also be the hardest thing you've ever done. That's why we need God and the model of his grace for our own marriages.

Why grace? That's the question this study will address along with many other challenges and joys we experience in our relationships.

God has a bride and that bride is his church. How does God treat us, his bride? With grace!

- He knows we don't get it right all the time and gives us a second chance.
- He gives us his favor even when we don't really deserve it.
- He looks beyond our weaknesses and sees our potential and worth.
- He loves us for who we are even when we mess up or in spite of what we do.

Grace keeps our love from growing weary, bitter, disappointed and mediocre. With God's grace, your marriage can be more than you dreamed it would be!

> **A special note to blended marriages and pre-married couples.**
>
> Blended families have many unique challenges, some completely out of your control. God's grace is custom made for those challenges. Keep your focus off the things over which you have little control and concentrate on the love that brought you together and God's grace that can keep you together.
>
> If you're coming up on your wedding, congratulations on investing your time to learn how to make God's grace the defining feature of your future marriage. We've given you an opportunity in every discussion time to customize this material to your pre-married status.

Whether you're at the beginning of your marriage, or you've been at it for a while; whether you're previously married or pre-married, it is our hope and prayer that you can gain some practical insights for your unique family situation. Since this material is taken from the timeless and well-proven truth of the Scriptures, these principles can be adapted to all kinds of family dynamics.

You are highly valued and we know that God can use you to implant his grace into your own life and marriage.

God bless you!

Because Every Family Matters,

Tim and Darcy

Dr. Tim and Darcy Kimmel

Session 1
What's Grace Got to Do with It?

Introduction:

God put marriage at the point position of his strategy for transferring his heart of love and mercy down through the ages.

The key to having a mutually satisfying marriage is contingent on our ability to maintain a passionate and empowering _____ connection with each other. Our onboard love can't pull this off on its own.

<u>The missing ingredient in marriages that struggle isn't love; it's grace!</u>

Love is what gets us married; **grace** is what keeps us married.

   I. We need grace to shore up our love because the love we bring to our marriage has the deck stacked against it.

      A. Trump Card: There are a lot of _____ that test our love.

      B. Trump Card: We're surrounded by a culture that prioritizes _____ over commitment.

      C. Trump Card: We encounter _____ which, although they are inevitable to ALL marriages, still manage to take us by surprise.

      D. Trump Card: We allow other _____ to receive the focus and affection we're supposed to reserve for each other.

      E. Trump Card: Our onboard _____ tends to corrode our love.

For help navigating a hectic, hurried life, try reading *Little House on the Freeway: Help for the Hurried Home*. (DVD study available too.)

Unfortunately, the relationship that needs grace the most is too often the one in which grace is _____ _____.

> *Be careful that none of you fails to respond to the grace which God gives, for if he does there can very easily spring up in him a bitter spirit which is not only bad in itself but can also poison the lives of many others.*
> —Hebrews 12:15 (PHILLIPS)

A. It's easy to miss the role of grace in our marriage when we limit the work of God's grace to salvation.

B. It's easy to miss the role of grace in our marriage because we often confuse grace with "_____."

C. It's easy to miss the role of grace in our marriage because we often limit our understanding of Christian marriage to the handful of passages in the Bible that unpack the "mechanics" of marriage.

D. Grace is giving your spouse something they _____ _____, but don't necessarily deserve.

> *Each of you should use whatever gift you have received to serve others, as faithful stewards of God's grace in its various forms.*
> —1 Peter 4:10

E. A grace-filled marriage is simply treating your spouse the way God treats you.

Conclusion:

God wants us to weave his heart of grace into our marriage and allow him to bring true beauty to the demanding and difficult chapters of our love story.

FROM AMERICA'S MOST TRUSTED AUTHORITY ON THE NUTRITIONAL CONTENT OF FOOD—
100 DELICIOUS, LOW FAT RECIPES
THAT WERE TESTED AGAIN AND AGAIN FOR GREAT TASTE

Try *Fish Soup Provençal,* which delivers all the flavors of sunny southern France, but the one thing it doesn't deliver is fat—a mere 2.1 grams per serving. Lighter than air and just as light on calories (only 160!), elegant *Mousse of Sole with Cucumber Sauce* is an appetizer fit for company. And a full-bodied Basque favorite, *Casserole of Red Snapper with Spinach and Potatoes,* is a complete low fat dinner that provides each member of the family with a healthful 29.5 grams of protein.

Corinne T. Netzer uses all the knowledge and expertise that made her sensational bestseller, *The Complete Book of Food Counts,* the #1 nutritional reference in America to create 100 low fat recipes bursting with flavor and glorious good health. From down-home catfish to delicious mako shark, *100 Low Fat Fish and Shellfish Recipes* lets you enjoy sumptuous guilt-free dining—whether you're watching your fat intake, counting calories, or just trying to maintain a healthy lifestyle.

NUTRITIONAL ANALYSES FOR EACH RECIPE INCLUDE:
• Fat grams • Calorie counts
• Carbohydrate grams • Cholesterol milligrams
• Sodium milligrams • Protein grams

US $5.99 / $7.99 CAN

ISBN 0-440-22352-0

Making This Yours

We hope you've had an opportunity to read chapter 1 of *Grace Filled Marriage*. Your enjoyment of this study and your takeaway value will be greatly enhanced by reading through the corresponding chapters of the book *Grace Filled Marriage*.

bit.ly/gracefilled

Getting It Started

1. Tell the group how long you've been married or together, where you got married, and how you felt about your new spouse the week after your wedding.

2. After you were together a while, which characteristics or quirks of yours surprised your mate?

> **In the event that none of your issues come to mind, here are a few ideas:**
>
> - Your annoying habits—or your lack of good habits
> - The way you save money—or the way you spend it
> - Your need to be early to events—or your consistent tardiness
> - The reality that you don't talk much—or that you won't stop talking
> - Your "neat freak" obsessions—or your sloppiness
> - How you load the dishwasher—or the fact that you didn't even know you had a dishwasher

3. Tim tells us that grace is "giving your spouse something they deeply need, but don't necessarily deserve" by treating each other the way God treats us. Did you grow up with parents who showed grace to each other? How has that affected your own relationship?

Taking It Deeper

1. 2 Corinthians 9:8 (ESV) says:

> *And God is able to make all grace abound to you, so that*
> *having all sufficiency in all things at all times, you may abound*
> *in every good work.*

What do you think about this idea of God's grace applying to more than salvation? Things like your marriage and relationships? If you treated your spouse the way God treats you, with grace, how would your relationship look different?

2. The author of Hebrews encourages us to respond to God's grace so that we don't get bitter and poison the lives of others.

> *Be careful that none of you fails to respond to the grace which*
> *God gives, for if he does there can very easily spring up in him*
> *a bitter spirit which is not only bad in itself but can also poison*
> *the lives of many others.*
> —Hebrews 12:15 (PHILLIPS)

What are some specific consequences of failing to respond to the grace God gives? How do these consequences apply to your marriage?

Bringing It Home

1. Married love can grow weary, stale, bruised, and even bitter. As you think about the Trump Cards that Tim talked about (adjustments, performance, inevitable setbacks, out-of-whack priorities, and onboard selfishness), which of these has given you the most challenges in your marriage?

How have you dealt with these difficulties?

2. Can you think of a few reasons you may struggle to show more grace in your marriage? Why do you think that happens? Can you or anyone in your group think of a Scripture verse that addresses the difficulty we may have in giving grace to our spouse?

3. How has this session challenged and/or confirmed your perceptions and assumptions about grace and/or marriage?

   Pre-Married Couples – How does this session apply to what you are dealing with in your countdown to marriage?

   Blended Couples – Share how this session applies to some of the unique complexities of blending two families.

Write it Down

As you commit to more grace in your own life and marriage, name one thing you learned in this session that you're going to put into practice this week. (Write this down before you dismiss.)

_____

_____

_____

_____

_____

_____

Take a moment to turn to your spouse or fiancé and share what you just wrote down. Commit to encouraging each other this week.

This is a time for you to pray as a couple. Use the prayer below to guide you. Go ahead and pray even if you're by yourself.

Prayer

Thank you, Father, for offering the same grace to our marriages as you offer to us. Grace is not natural to me so I really need your help as I try to apply it to the person you have given me to love for the rest of my life. Thank you for never leaving me on my own but staying with me all the way. Amen.

Prayer Requests:

_____

_____

_____

_____

_____

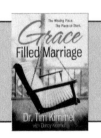

Read:

Please read chapters 2 and 3 of the book *Grace Filled Marriage* to get the most out of the upcoming session. If you haven't done so already, please also read chapter 1.

Watch...

...this short video to learn more about Grace as the missing element in many marriages.

*(many thanks to those who responded to this video and made this DVD study of **Grace Filled Marriage** possible)*

bit.ly/gracesaves

Session 2
Marriage Through the Lens of God's Grace

Introduction:

Our personal point of view plays a huge role in how we view and treat our spouse. It determines whether we even have a chance to truly maintain close and intimate heart connection.

> *Therefore be imitators of God, as beloved children.*
> —Ephesians 5:1 (ESV)

> *And God is able to make all grace abound to you, so that having all sufficiency in all things at all times, you may abound in every good work.*
> —2 Corinthians 9:8 (ESV)

I. **If we want to enjoy a grace-filled marriage, it's essential that we honestly acknowledge and confess some of the graceless ways we often view our spouse.**

   A. We all look at our spouse through lenses that determine our attitudes and actions towards them.

   B. The unfortunate truth is that we often choose to look at our spouse through lenses that guarantee we won't be able to enjoy the active presence and working power of God's grace in our marriage, let alone maintain intimate heart connection with them.

   1. The _____ Lens

> *Do nothing out of selfish ambition or vain conceit. Rather, in humility value others above yourselves, not looking to your own interests but each of you to the interests of others.*
> —Philippians 2:3-4

   2. The _____ ____ Lens

Lie 1: Based on all Christ did for you, you owe him.

Lie 2: The way you pay Jesus back is by being a good Christian.

Lie 3: If you obey Jesus more, you'll get more of his love; if you don't, don't expect much in return. It's only fair.

> *He does not treat us as our sins deserve or repay us according to our iniquities.*
> —Psalm 103:10

> *For I am convinced that neither death nor life, neither angels nor demons, neither the present nor the future, nor any powers, neither height nor depth, nor anything else in all creation, will separate us from the love of God that is in Christ Jesus our Lord.*
> —Romans 8:38-39

3. The _____ Lens

> *But be doers of the word, and not hearers only, deceiving yourselves.*
> —James 1:22 (ESV)

C. These three lenses share something in common: they're all rooted in our pride. God's grace can't operate within prideful people because pride is the antithesis of his heart. Therefore, pride _____ God from working through us on behalf of others.

> *…God opposes the proud, but gives grace to the humble.*
> —James 4:6 (ESV)

A *Me* perspective, *Love If* perspective, and *Pious* perspective dishonor the work of the _____ in our lives and contradict the nature of God's heart.

II. **If we want to enjoy a grace-filled marriage, it's essential that we allow God to _____ the way we view our spouse into the way he views us.**

A. God showed the true nature of his heart, as well as the kind of love he wants us to enjoy in our marriages, when he proposed his intention to have a lasting relationship with us…at the cross.

B. God always meant for his grace to reconfigure our perspectives, fill us with his presence, and free us to operate in his power.

C. We can try to love each other in our own power (limited as it is), but _____ will only show up in our marriage when we get our pride and control out of the way and surrender ourselves completely to the power of God.

Conclusion:

Until we let God's grace become the lens through which we view our spouse, all of our self-powered efforts will fall short.

Making This Yours

How did it go with implementing a practical application from the previous session? Share your successes and failures, because we learn from both.

What was one insight, principle, or illustration that stuck with you as you did your reading this week in *Grace Filled Marriage*?

Getting It Started

1. Let's get vulnerable here! We all struggle with looking through the wrong lens in our marriage. Which lens do you struggle with the most (the Me Lens, the Love If Lens, or the Pious Lens)? And while we're being candid, share an example of how you look through that lens.

2. What is the "credit card" issue that you seem to focus on all too often? Can you think of a few ways that this hyper focus on a flaw has kept you and your spouse from nurturing your heart connection as a couple?

3. Tim says, "To have a grace-filled marriage, it's essential that we allow God to transform the way we view our spouse into the way he views us." How do you anticipate that this grace perspective will draw you closer to your spouse?

Taking It Deeper

1. Too many times, we know what we should do to treat our spouse the way God treats us but we just don't do it.

> But be doers of the word, and not hearers only, deceiving yourselves.
> —James 1:22 (ESV)

Without relying on a lot of rationalization, what keeps us from doing the right thing?

How much does pride play into your refusal to love your spouse with Christ's love?

> *God opposes the proud, but gives grace to the humble.*
> —James 4:6 (ESV)

How are you going to appropriate God's power to overcome pride with grace?

2. How does God's proposal to you to be his spouse change the way you view his love for you?

> *Husbands, love your wives,*
> *just as Christ loved the church and gave himself up for her.*
> —Ephesians 5:25

In what ways does God's personal love for you inspire your love for your spouse?

Bringing It Home

1. Think about the lenses you struggle with most (Me, Love If, Pious). How will your behavior change as a result of knowing your perspective is flawed?

2. What point do you think Tim and Darcy were trying to make with the balloon illustration?

3. How has this session challenged and/or confirmed your perceptions and assumptions about grace and/or marriage?

   Pre-Married Couples - How does this session apply to what you are dealing with in the countdown to marriage?

   Blended Couples – Share how this session applies to some of the unique complexities of blending two families.

Write it Down

As you commit to more grace in your own life and marriage, name one thing you learned in this session that you're going to put into practice this week. (Write this down before you dismiss.)

_____

_____

_____

_____

_____

_____

Take a moment to turn to your spouse or fiancé and share what you just wrote down. Commit to encouraging each other this week.

This is a time for you to pray as a couple. Use the prayer below to guide you. Go ahead and pray even if you're by yourself.

Prayer

Dear Jesus, Thank you for climbing up on that cross and declaring your love for me. Thank you for giving me something that I desperately needed but didn't deserve. I want to love my spouse the same way you love me. Please help me to look through the grace lens as I love the mate you have blessed me with. Amen.

Prayer Requests:

_____

_____

_____

_____

_____

Read:

Please read chapter 4 of the book *Grace Filled Marriage* in order to get the most out of the upcoming session.

Listen...

......to this audio message from Tim to learn more about what grace is and what it isn't.

Download for free with code: GFMSTUDY1

bit.ly/gracelistaudio

God's Grace and a Secure Love

Introduction:

Marriage relationships don't suddenly blow out on their own. A major downturn in a marriage is usually the result of a slow leak in the relationship over a protracted period of time.

It's easier to detect and patch slow leaks in marriage when we allow God's heart of grace to redefine our love and then let it frame our attitudes and actions on a daily basis.

> *I'll remove the stone heart from your body and replace it with a heart that's God-willed, not self-willed.*
> —Ezekiel 36:26 (MSG)

I. **A grace-filled marriage is easier to maintain when we know exactly what grace looks like lived out in a heart connected relationship.**

 A. Making God's grace the default mode of our marriage requires more than a nice behavioral checklist—especially in the grittier moments of our lives as couples.

 B. A _____-_____ view of God's grace gives us the philosophical starting point, a strategic path to follow, and specific tactics to carry out.

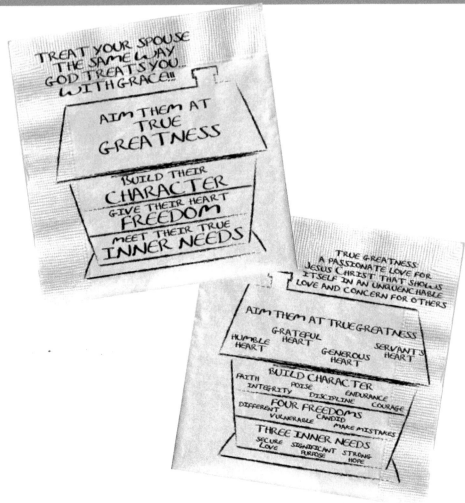

God's grace ministers to our hearts at four levels:

- He sees our truest needs (inner needs).
- He knows our deepest longings (freedom).
- He understands our greatest challenges (character).
- He envisions our highest potential (true greatness).

Because we're supposed to be a reflection of him in our marriage, we can use this napkin model as a template to minister to our spouse's heart the same way.

II. **Grace-filled marriages operate in constant awareness of each spouse's driving inner need for security, significance, and strength—and a commitment to meet these needs** _____.

   A. God's grace consistently coaxes our spouse's heart towards _____.

> And let us consider how we may spur one another on toward love and good deeds.
> —Hebrews 10:24

A commitment to meeting each other's driving inner needs consistently raises the spiritual, emotional, and even financial stock value of our marriage.

III. **God's heart of grace inclines us to build a** _____ _____ **into our spouse's heart.**

   A. Our commitment to love our spouse is easier to keep on target when we have a clear definition of love guiding us.

> **Love is:**
> the commitment of my will
> to your needs and best interest
> regardless of the cost.

> God demonstrates his own love for us in this:
> While we were still sinners, Christ died for us.
> —Romans 5:8

   B. Our spouse feels secure when we _____ them.

- This doesn't mean that we tolerate or accommodate clear areas of sin.

- We must avoid the toxic poison of criticism.

- We must avoid the toxic poison of comparison.

> *See to it that no one misses the grace of God and that no bitter root grows up to cause trouble and defile many.*
> —Hebrews 12:15

C. Our spouse feels secure when we maintain a strong _____ with the passions of their heart.

> *Be happy with those who are happy, and weep with those who weep. Live in harmony with each other.*
> *Don't be too proud to enjoy the company of ordinary people.*
> *And don't think you know it all!*
> —Romans 12:15-16 (NLT)

D. Our spouse feels secure when we show them consistent _____.

Conclusion

God protects our love when we allow his grace to become the default mode of our relationship. His grace inclines us to meet our spouse's driving inner needs; in particular, their need for a secure love.

We build a secure love into our spouse by accepting them as a wonderful and unique creation, encouraging them in things that have captured their heart, and prioritizing the gift of affection.

---

5 Ways to Help Build a Secure Love in Your Spouse

1. Frequently tell your spouse what you like about them.
2. Encourage them to cultivate supportive friendships.
3. Remember them in a special (not necessarily expensive) way on key holidays and occasions.
4. Show interest in their job by asking specific questions about their day.
5. Praise them in public and in front of the children.

Making This Yours

How did it go with implementing a practical application from the previous session? Share your successes and failures, because we learn from both.

What was one insight, principle, or illustration that stuck with you as you did your reading this week in *Grace Filled Marriage*?

Getting It Started

1. Can you think of another area of your life where the daily requirements make more sense when you keep the "big picture" in mind? How are you motivated by a big picture when it comes to the tactics that aren't much fun? How have you used this principle with your children?

2. Did you grow up feeling a secure love? Whether your answer is yes or no, how has that background aided or handicapped you as you try to meet that need in your spouse?

3. We all have areas in our relationship that could use some work. Are there some slow leaks in your relationship that a secure love could patch?

4. What are some issues that your spouse has accepted about you? Has their acceptance changed your view of yourself? Of them?

Taking It Deeper

1. Love obviously has a price tag attached to it. As you look at the Kimmels' definition of love and the Scripture below, share a time when someone showed you this kind of love. How did that demonstration of love impact you?

> **Love is:**
> the commitment of my will
> to your needs and best interest
> regardless of the cost.

> *And let us consider how we may spur one another on*
> *toward love and good deeds.*
> —Hebrews 10:24

2. The verses below promise that when we know Christ as our Savior, we don't need to worry about God withholding his love and grace from us. We are securely loved.

> *My sheep listen to my voice; I know them, and they follow me.*
> *I give them eternal life, and they shall never perish; no one will*
> *snatch them out of my hand.*
> —John 10:27-28

How does God's unfailing love make you feel? Share a few ways that your spouse makes you feel securely loved.

Bringing It Home

1. Tim shared the house/napkin model for grace-based relationships with us. This illustration will be something that we refer back to repeatedly in the study. The best way to learn something is to teach it, so this week, take the house/napkin and begin to explain it to someone—maybe your child, a friend, your pastor, or you can even practice on your spouse. If you're very courageous, ask them if they'll let you practice teaching it a few more times as we learn more about each level.

Watch:

To see an animated version of the house model applied to parenting, go to:

bit.ly/whatisGBP

2. Try to go on a date this week or just set aside a few quiet moments together with your spouse. Ask them to answer these questions for you:

- What is one thing you love to do that you wish I would occasionally do with you?

- What is one thing you love to do that you wish I would encourage you to do more?

- Now take this information and determine to use it in a way that builds a more secure love in them. Who knows, you may even have fun in the process!

3. How has this session challenged and/or confirmed your perceptions and assumptions about grace and/or marriage?

Pre-Married Couples – How does this session apply to what you are dealing with in your countdown to marriage?

Blended Couples – Share how this session applies to some of the unique complexities of blending two families.

Write it Down

As you commit to more grace in your own life and marriage, name one thing you learned in this session that you're going to put into practice this week. (Write this down before you dismiss.)

_____

_____

_____

_____

_____

_____

Take a moment to turn to your spouse or fiancé and share what you just wrote down. Commit to encouraging each other this week.

This is a time for you to pray as a couple. Use the prayer below to guide you. Go ahead and pray even if you're by yourself.

Prayer

Lord, I want to coax my spouse's heart toward full by helping to meet their driving inner need to feel securely loved. Thank you for setting an example by accepting us and knowing the passions of our hearts. Would you make me keenly aware this week of ways I can encourage a secure love in my mate? Thank you. Amen.

Prayer Requests:

_____

_____

_____

_____

_____

_____

_____

Read:

Please reread pages 74-86 (Grace-Filled Sex) of the book *Grace Filled Marriage* in order to get the most out of the upcoming session.

Discover...

......your key motivators and passions by taking the *Flag Page* assessment with your spouse. Plan a date night to discuss the results with each other. This tool will give you a whole new perspective on how to communicate effectively with one another.

bit.ly/flagpage

Session 4
Grace-Filled Sex

Introduction:

It is vital to our heart connection as couples that we graciously and enthusiastically maintain a healthy view of sex and honor its greater role in marriage.

Sex allows a husband and wife to experience a physical, emotional, and spiritual connection that's in a league of its own.

> *Now the man and his wife were both naked,*
> *but they felt no shame.*
> —Genesis 2:25 (NLT)

I. **God's transforming work of grace gives us the power to overcome the standard ways sex is often mishandled in marriages.**

    A. When our focus is on ourselves, it's easy to end up using or viewing sex in ways God never meant for us to view it or use it.

- Some people see sex as an
  _____.

- Some people use sex to
  _____ their spouse.

- Some people use sex to _____ their spouse.

    B. When our focus is on ourselves, we can end up dealing with sex in ways that are degrading to our spouse and foreign to a heart tempered by God's grace.

- Some people _____ sex from their spouse.

- Some people _____ their spouse of sex.

> *The thief comes only to steal and kill and destroy;*
> *I came that they may have life and have it abundantly.*
> —John 10:10 (ESV)

Jesus paid a huge price so that we can move beyond the misuse of his gift of sex.

> *Therefore, if anyone is in Christ, he is a new creation.*
> *The old has passed away; behold, the new has come.*
> —2 Corinthians 5:17 (ESV)

II. A heart defined by God's grace sees sex within the marriage as a magnanimous way to honor and _____ our spouse.

    A. Grace-based intimacy is about giving with _____ and receiving with joy.

    B. Grace-based intimacy is about maintaining a holy _____ for our spouse as well as taking _____ in being needed.

> *Do not deprive each other of sexual relations, unless you both*
> *agree to refrain from sexual intimacy for a limited time so you*
> *can give yourselves more completely to prayer. Afterward, you*
> *should come together again so that Satan won't be able to*
> *tempt you because of your lack of self-control.*
> —1 Corinthians 7:5 (NLT)

    C. A grace-filled attitude towards sex gives a couple enormous protection and security in the midst of a sexually contaminated culture.

> The husband should fulfill his wife's sexual needs, and the wife
> should fulfill her husband's needs. The wife gives authority over
> her body to her husband, and the husband gives
> authority over his body to his wife.
> —1 Corinthians 7:3-4 (NLT)

Conclusion

The grace Jesus offers through the cross gives us the power to get healing from the past as well as to secure our heart connection with each other when it comes to this vital, private, and God-ordained dimension of our love story.

Making This Yours

How did it go with implementing a practical application from the previous session? Share your successes and failures, because we learn from both.

What was one insight, principle, or illustration that stuck with you as you did your reading this week in *Grace Filled Marriage*?

Getting It Started

1. There's no denying that we are shaped by our upbringing, background, and experience when it comes to the area of sexual intimacy in our marriage. Share some of the ways you were influenced in this area before you got married. Positively, and if you're comfortable, negatively.

2. The Kimmels make it very clear that a "convenience store" attitude of availability is not a license to take advantage or to demand. With that in mind, how can an attitude of availability reflect God's grace and build a more secure love in marriage?

3. How did you or how will you explain to your children why God designed sex to be a part of a happy and healthy marriage?

Taking It Deeper

1. Read this famous love passage from the Scriptures and apply it to grace-filled sex in a marriage.

> *Love is patient and kind. Love is not jealous or boastful or proud or rude. It does not demand its own way. It is not irritable, and it keeps no record of being wronged. It does not rejoice about injustice but rejoices whenever the truth wins out. Love never gives up, never loses faith, is always hopeful, and endures through every circumstance. Prophecy and speaking in unknown languages and special knowledge will become useless. But love will last forever!*
> —1 Corinthians 13:4-8 (NLT)

2. No verse in the Bible is a throwaway verse, certainly none regarding the first married couple. Why do you think God included this verse in the Scriptures?

> *The man and his wife were both naked, but they felt no shame.*
> —Genesis 2:25 (NLT)

Think out loud about some of the reasons that they were not ashamed. How can some of those reasons carry over into our own "taste of Eden"? How does this work toward a more secure love in a marriage relationship?

Bringing It Home

1. Talk about some ways to apply grace to offset some of the sexual attitudes or actions that may need adjusting in a marriage (obligation, manipulation, punishment, demanding, defrauding). What would that grace look like? (For example, the next time your spouse feels like their behavior has blown the chance of romance for the week, surprise them with a romantic encounter.)

2. Tim says that "a grace-filled attitude towards sex gives a couple enormous protection and security in the midst of a sexually contaminated culture." What are some sexual minefields out there in our daily lives? How can a grace-filled attitude in our intimate life inoculate us and our spouse against those traps? What are some tangible ways you're going to translate those gracious attitudes (enthusiasm, joy, holy desire, delight) into actions this week?

3. How has this session challenged and/or confirmed your perceptions and assumptions about grace and/or marriage?

   Pre-Married Couples – How does this session apply to what you are dealing with in your countdown to marriage?

   Blended Couples – Share how this session applies to some of the unique complexities of blending two families.

Write it Down

As you commit to more grace in your own life and marriage, name one thing you learned in this session that you're going to put into practice this week. (Write this down before you dismiss.)

_____

_____

_____

_____

Take a moment to turn to your spouse or fiancé and share what you just wrote down. Commit to encouraging each other this week.

This is a time for you to pray as a couple. Use the prayer below to guide you. Go ahead and pray even if you're by yourself.

Prayer

Father, I thank you for the gift of sexual intimacy with my spouse and for the way it can help meet the need for a secure love in them. Please give me your grace as I seek to honor and serve my mate in this area. Help me to overcome the negative influence of my past and the selfish habits of the present. I ask these things in the name of your Son, the generous lover of my soul. Amen.

Prayer Requests:

_____

_____

_____

Read:

Please read chapters 5-6 of the book *Grace Filled Marriage* in order to get the most out of the upcoming session.

There are times when the money runs out before the month does. Here are a few dating ideas that don't cost a lot.

Creative Dating

1. Give your spouse a foot rub
2. Put together a puzzle in front of the fireplace
3. Take an early morning canoe ride
4. Have a candlelight picnic in the backyard
5. Serve breakfast in bed
6. Reminisce through your wedding photos
7. Take a walk in the rain under a big umbrella
8. Give your spouse a full body massage
9. Watch a movie with a classic love story together
10. Go swimming in the moonlight
11. Build a snowman
12. Take a walk as you watch the sunset

Listen...

...to Tim and Darcy as they discuss the importance of a healthy sexual relationship in your marriage in this radio interview on **Family Life Today.**

bit.ly/graceradio

Introduction:

Marriage is the ideal setting for both mining and refining our potential as individuals.

Marriage is also capable of blunting everything good about us. It depends on how much we're willing to let God's gracious heart of hope, mercy, and forgiveness flow through us to our spouse.

**I.   God's grace inspires us to meet our spouse's need for a
   _____ purpose.**

People want to matter. They need to matter. They were made to matter.

> *For we are his handiwork, created in Christ Jesus to do good works, which God prepared in advance for us to do.*
> —Ephesians 2:10

A.   Our spouse feels a significant purpose when we
   _____ them.

> *Do not let any unwholesome talk come out of your mouths, but only what is helpful for building others up according to their needs, that it may benefit those who listen.*
> —Ephesians 4:29

B.   Our spouse feels a significant purpose when we give them
   our _____.

> *Keep me as the apple of your eye; hide me in the shadow of your wings.*
> —Psalm 17:8

C.   Our spouse feels a significant purpose when we gracefully
   _____ them.

> *Those whom I love I rebuke and discipline.*
> *So be earnest and repent.*
> —Revelation 3:19

> *A gentle answer deflects anger,*
> *but harsh words make tempers flare.*
> —Proverbs 15:1 (NLT)

---

5 Ways to Help Build a Significant Purpose in Your Spouse

1. Entrust your spouse with your vision for the future.

2. Pray for your spouse regularly.

3. Listen with your heart before you disagree or criticize your spouse.

4. Praise your spouse in front of the kids.

5. Use the two-for-one rule. For every negative topic you must discuss, spend twice as long talking about something positive.

VI. God's grace inspires us to meet our spouse's need for a
_____ _____.

The biggest obstacle to building a strong hope into our spouse is fear.

> *Don't worry about anything; instead, pray about everything. Tell God what you need, and thank him for all he has done. Then you will experience God's peace, which exceeds anything we can understand. His peace will guard your hearts and minds as you live in Christ Jesus.*
> —Philippians 4:6-7 (NLT)

A. Our spouse feels a strong hope when we encourage their God-given _____.

When we empower our spouse to harness their abilities, we strengthen ourselves as a team.

B. Our spouse feels a strong hope when we encourage them toward great

_____.

Grace compels us to bring vision and tender inspiration to the role we play as our spouse's mentor.

C. Our spouse feels a strong hope when we help them live a great _____.

A couple can't live a life of genuine faith without being willing to follow God into places they've never been before—trusting him all the way.

A spiritually convenient and comfortable environment doesn't incline a couple towards a frontline faith—nor does it galvanize their relationship with each other.

> With all this going for us, my dear, dear friends, stand your ground. And don't hold back. Throw yourselves into the work of the Master, confident that nothing you do for him is a waste of time or effort.
> —1 Corinthians 15:58 (MSG)

5 Ways to Help Build a Strong Hope in Your Spouse

1. When they feel like a loser, treat them like a winner and watch them act like one.

2. Stay out of consumer debt, so you two are free to answer God's call to some great adventure.

3. Give each other daily and generous hugs, kisses, and words of love.

4. Say "I believe in you" when they're having trouble believing in themselves.

5. Mail a card to them at work or home that says they're the greatest mom/dad. Have all the kids sign it.

Conclusion

Grace-filled married couples are deliberate about building a secure love, a significant purpose, and a strong hope into each other.

> *"I said to the man who stood at the gate of the year, 'Give me a light that I may tread safely into the unknown.'*
> *And he replied, 'Go into the darkness and put your hand into the hand of God. That shall be to you better than light and safer than a known way.'"*
> —Minnie Louise Haskins

This quote is fitting advice for all of us as we bring our personal inadequacies and fears to the role of building a secure love, significant purpose, and strong hope into our spouse.

Making This Yours

How did it go with implementing a practical application from the previous session? Share your successes and failures, because we learn from both.

What was one insight, principle, or illustration that stuck with you as you did your reading this week in *Grace Filled Marriage*?

Getting It Started

1. Tim likes to say that "you're either doubled or halved on your wedding day." How were you doubled on your wedding day? What effect has your marriage had on your sense of purpose and hope? Do you know of anyone that was halved on their wedding day? How did that diminish the sense of purpose or hope in their life?

2. Identify some of the significant purposes for which God has equipped you. How has your spouse affirmed and admonished you in these? What are some things you could be doing to help your spouse fill their need for a significant purpose?

3. Helping our spouse live a great adventure builds into them a strong hope. Share with the group a time when your mate helped you take a risk, face an unknown, and/or overcome a fear and how it made you stronger, more confident, and hopeful.

Taking It Deeper

1. A sense of a significant purpose and a strong hope can help us weather the inevitable storms of life and relationships. Look at the passage below and expound on Paul's progression and reasoning that results in a hope that "does not disappoint." Can you tell about a time when you actually experienced this metamorphosis from tribulation to hope?

> *And not only this, but we also exult in our tribulations, knowing that tribulation brings about perseverance; and perseverance, proven character; and proven character, hope; and hope does not disappoint, because the love of God has been poured out within our hearts through the Holy Spirit who was given to us.*
> —Romans 5:3-5 (NASB)

2. Fear can hold our hearts and our homes hostage, robbing us of purpose and hope.

> *Don't worry about anything; instead, pray about everything. Tell God what you need, and thank him for all he has done. Then you will experience God's peace, which exceeds anything we can understand. His peace will guard your hearts and minds as you live in Christ Jesus*
> —Philippians 4:6-7 (NLT)

How does this passage admonish us to address our fears?

Christ's gracious work for us on the cross should give us the ability to face our fears more effectively. Tell about a time when you allowed God to replace your fear with peace. How did that affect your sense of hope and significance?

Bringing It Home

1. Let's get vulnerable here. Think about some of the discouraging things you say to your spouse. What affirming words will you replace those unwholesome words with this week? What affirming words would you like your spouse to say to you this week? Practice this at home.

2. What are some of your major distractions when it comes to giving attention to your spouse? What are you going to do to change this? Is there an area in which you'd like your spouse to show you some special attention? If you could plan an evening just for the two of you, what would you want the evening to include and exclude?

3. How has this session challenged and/or confirmed your perceptions and assumptions about grace and/or marriage?

Pre-Married Couples – How does this session apply to what you are dealing with in your countdown to marriage?

Blended Couples – Share how this session applies to some of the unique complexities of blending two families.

Write it Down

As you commit to more grace in your own life and marriage, name one thing you learned in this session that you're going to put into practice this week. (Write this down before you dismiss.)

_____

_____

_____

_____

_____

_____

Take a moment to turn to your spouse or fiancé and share what you just wrote down. Commit to encouraging each other this week.

This is a time for you to pray as a couple. Use the prayer below to guide you. Go ahead and pray even if you're by yourself.

Prayer

Lord, thank you for the intrinsic value that you place on all of us as your children. Please help me with my words and actions to communicate a sense of significance to my spouse. And where would our hope be without the cross of Calvary? As I do what I can to fill my mate with a strong hope, fill me with the hope that finds its power in the Gospel. Amen.

Prayer Requests:

_____

_____

_____

_____

_____

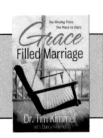

Read:

Please read chapters 7-8 of the book *Grace Filled Marriage* in order to get the most out of the upcoming session.

Listen...

...to these **Family Matters Minutes** that deliver powerful marriage tips in under 60 seconds.

bit.ly/fmmmarriage

Session 6
The Freedom within a Grace-Filled Marriage

Introduction:

One of the most effective delivery systems for a grace-filled relationship is a marriage that deliberately sets each other's hearts free.

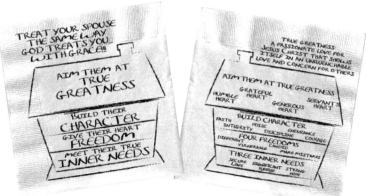

> *You will know the truth, and the truth will set you free.*
> —John 8:32

Freedom isn't the license to do whatever we want (that's anarchy), but rather the ability to do what God created us to do without artificially imposed restraints.

I.   Grace-filled spouses give each other the freedom to be

   _____.

   A.   Grace doesn't marginalize a spouse for things that are unique features of their physical, intellectual, or personality makeup.

   B.   Grace doesn't make _____ matters out of non-moral matters or biblical issues out of non-biblical issues.

Read *The High Cost of High Control*:

We all have a tendency to want to control our spouse. Whether you're the one controlling or being controlled, you'll want to read this book that can set you free.

II. Grace-filled spouses give each other the freedom to be

_____.

A. Grace doesn't leverage a spouse's weaknesses against them.

> *Let your conversation be always full of grace, seasoned with salt, so that you may know how to answer everyone.*
> —Colossians 4:6

B. Grace-filled couples provide a _____ place for their spouse to process the more fragile features of their heart.

> *Cry for help and you'll find it's grace and more grace.*
> —Isaiah 30:19 (MSG)

III. Grace-filled spouses give each other the freedom to be

_____.

A. Grace provides a safe outlet for the concerns churning within our spouse's heart.

> *Let us then approach the throne of grace with confidence, so that we may receive mercy and find grace to help us in our time of need.*
> —Hebrews 4:16

B. Giving freedom to reveal our hearts to each other should always be done respectfully.

> *Get rid of all bitterness, rage and anger, brawling and slander, along with every form of malice.*
> —Ephesians 4:31

> *See to it that no one falls short of the grace of God and that no bitter root grows up to cause trouble and defile many.*
> —Hebrews 12:15

IV. Grace-filled spouses give each other the freedom to process their _____.

The standard human reaction to a misdemeanor in a marriage is annoyance and voicing frustration, with a little quid pro quo payback thrown in.

> *Good sense makes one slow to anger,*
> *and it is his glory to overlook an offense.*
> —Proverbs 19:11 (ESV)

The standard human reaction to a felony against your heart is rage, condemnation, and a desire to _____ them.

A. God's grace calls us to maintain a righteous justice towards our spouse's sinful actions, while at the same time never letting go of a _____ _____ toward them as a person.

> *Brothers, if anyone is caught in any transgression, you who are spiritual should restore him in a spirit of gentleness. Keep watch on yourself, lest you too be tempted. Bear one another's burdens, and so fulfill the law of Christ.*
> —Galatians 6:1-2 (ESV)

> *Godly sorrow brings repentance that leads to salvation and leaves no regret, but worldly sorrow brings death.*
> —2 Corinthians 7:10

B. Our own experience as people in desperate need of God's grace should _____ us as we consider our response to our spouse's mistakes.

> *My brothers and sisters, if one of you should wander from the truth and someone should bring him back, remember this: Whoever turns a sinner from the error of his way will save him from death and cover over a multitude of sins.*
> —James 5:19-20

Conclusion:

We infuse the fresh air of grace into our marriage when we give our spouse the freedom to be different, vulnerable, candid, and to grow past their mistakes.

Giving these freedoms is counterintuitive to the human heart. They're only possible when we let God's grace do a transforming work in our own heart.

Making This Yours

How did it go with implementing a practical application from the previous session? Share your successes and failures, because we learn from both.

What was one insight, principle, or illustration that stuck with you as you did your reading this week in *Grace Filled Marriage*?

Getting It Started

1. Talk about a time when you were especially vulnerable and someone (your spouse, a friend, another family member) gave you the freedom to be fragile and exposed. How did that make you feel about your circumstances and about that other person?

2. Tim points out the difference between candor and honesty. Can you think of a time when you were brutally honest as opposed to candid with your spouse? How did they respond? How do you think grace-filled candor could have changed the outcome?

3. When two become one, we share the fallout of each other's poor choices and sinful behavior. Look at the following short list of bad decisions and list out some of the possible collective consequences in a marriage (you may want to add a few of your own scenarios to the list):

   - Poor financial management

   - Neglected commitments with children

   - Irresponsible performance at work

   - Lackadaisical attitude toward church

How can you extend grace to your spouse while you're living under the consequences of poor choices?

Taking It Deeper

1. Look at Christ's invitation in Matthew 11, offering rest and freedom.

> *Are you tired? Worn out? Burned out on religion? Come to me. Get away with me and you'll recover your life. I'll show you how to take a real rest. Walk with me and work with me—watch how I do it. Learn the unforced rhythms of grace. I won't lay anything heavy or ill-fitting on you. Keep company with me and you'll learn to live freely and lightly.*
> —Matthew 11:28-30 (MSG)

How do his words appeal to you in your personal life? In your marriage?

As you read through these verses again, what does Christ suggest you do to experience his rest and freedom?

2. There are many things that can hurt us and tick us off in marriage. Grace calls us to maintain a righteous justice and a holy mercy when it comes to processing our spouse's mistakes. The way we respond to these challenging circumstances many times determines how much damage they will do to our relationship. Listen to Paul's advice on how to deal with these difficulties.

> *Let all bitterness and wrath and anger and clamor and slander be put away from you, along with all malice. Be kind to one another, tender-hearted, forgiving each other, just as God in Christ also has forgiven you.*
> —Ephesians 4:31-32 (NASB)

How can we relate what he says to our own marriage? Why should we do these things? What keeps us from following these guidelines?

Bringing It Home

1. If you had to name a few things that are unique (goofy, quirky, weird) about your spouse, what would they be? What can you do to give your spouse more freedom to be uniquely who God created them to be?

2. Would you say that your relationship has been characterized by candor in the past? As you move forward in a grace-filled marriage, what needs to change in this area so that you and your spouse have a more honorable exchange of concerns and issues of the heart? Remember that grace-filled candor builds up, not tears down; heals, not harms; cleanses, not curses.

   Which suggestion will you own this week?

3. How has this session challenged and/or confirmed your perceptions and assumptions about grace and/or marriage?

   Pre-Married Couples – How does this session apply to what you are dealing with in your countdown to marriage?

   Blended Couples – Share how this session applies to some of the unique complexities of blending two families.

Write it Down

As you commit to more grace in your own life and marriage, name one thing you learned in this session that you're going to put into practice this week. (Write this down before you dismiss.)

_____

_____

_____

_____

_____

_____

Take a moment to turn to your spouse or fiancé and share what you just wrote down. Commit to encouraging each other this week.

This is a time for you to pray as a couple. Use the prayer below to guide you. Go ahead and pray even if you're by yourself.

Prayer

Oh Father, thank you so much for celebrating who you made us to be, for wrapping your arms around our hurts and inadequacies, for listening to the cries of our heart, and for extending your grace when we fall short. I want to be like you with my mate but I know I can only do that in your power. Please fill me with your Holy Spirit as I try to be more of a picture of you in my marriage. Amen.

Prayer Requests:

_____

_____

_____

_____

_____

Read:

Please read chapter 9 of the book *Grace Filled Marriage* in order to get the most out of the upcoming session.

Listen...

...to this message from Tim as he describes the importance of giving these same four freedoms to our children.

Download for free with code: GFMSTUDY1

bit.ly/gbfaudio

The Character of a Grace-Filled Marriage

Introduction:

If marriage is comparable to anything, it's like a marathon—often uphill—with ongoing challenges and demands that are simply part of two people taking on the race of life as a team.

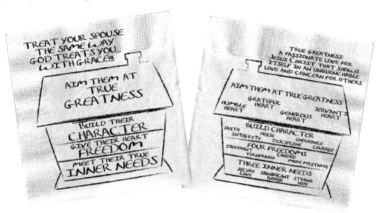

> *Do you not know that in a race all the runners run, but only one gets the prize? Run in such a way as to get the prize.*
> —1 Corinthians 9:24

If we want a marriage that runs the race of life strong and ultimately finishes well, we have to be committed to keeping our core character muscles strong both individually and as a couple—until death us do part.

I. God's grace encourages couples to maintain the character muscle of _____.

    A. God takes great pleasure when people who have received his gift of salvation go on to _____ him with their daily lives.

> *Without faith it is impossible to please God, because anyone who comes to him must believe that he exists and that he rewards those who earnestly seek him.*
> —Hebrews 11:6

B. People who trust God with their daily lives are naturally inclined to _____ him.

...you will flee even when no one is pursuing you.
—Leviticus 26:17

II. **God's grace encourages couples to maintain the character muscle of _____.**

A. Although our culture, our fears, and pride often encourage us to take moral shortcuts, the loss of God's pleasure is extremely tough on couples who take that path.

B. If we want to enjoy God's peace and _____, we need to be driven by uncompromised moral convictions.

...he swears to his own hurt and does not change.
—Psalm 15:4b (NASB)

III. **God's grace encourages couples to maintain the character muscle of _____.**

A. Poised couples avoid the _____ that make them fragile, destructive, irresponsible, or irrelevant.

Do not be overrighteous, neither be overwise–why destroy
yourself? Do not be overwicked, and do not be a fool–why die
before your time? It is good to grasp the one and not let go of
the other. Whoever fears God will avoid all extremes.
—Ecclesiastes 7:16-18

"I have the right to do anything," you say–but not everything is
beneficial. "I have the right to do anything"–but not
everything is constructive."
—1 Corinthians 10:23

B. Poise is a "keen sense of the appropriate." It helps keep our heart and our marriage in _____.

IV. God's grace encourages couples to maintain the character muscle of _____.

A. Disciplines are the boundaries we place around our strengths in order to maximize their

_____.

B. When God's grace has transformed our heart, it motivates us to take full advantage of all the good things he's given us to work with.

V. God's grace encourages couples to maintain the character muscle of _____.

A. God's grace helps couples to be there for each other throughout the marathon of their marriage.

> *May the God who gives endurance and encouragement give you the same attitude of mind toward each other that Christ Jesus had, so that with one mind and one voice you may glorify the God and Father of our Lord Jesus Christ.*
> —Romans 15:5-6

B. Our power to endure is found in the gracious work of Jesus on our behalf.

> *Since we are surrounded by such a great cloud of witnesses, let us throw off everything that hinders and the sin that so easily entangles. And let us run with perseverance the race marked out for us, fixing our eyes on Jesus, the pioneer and perfecter of faith. For the joy set before him he endured the cross, scorning its shame, and sat down at the right hand of the throne of God. Consider him who endured such opposition from sinners, so that you will not grow weary and lose heart.*
> —Hebrews 12:1-3

VI. God's grace encourages couples to maintain the character muscle of _____.

A. Grace-filled couples refuse to let their fears define their relationship or their commitment to finishing the race God has given them to run.

> *My dear brothers and sisters, stand firm. Let nothing move you. Always give yourselves fully to the work of the Lord, because you know that your labor in the Lord is not in vain.*
> —1 Corinthians 15:58

B. Grace-filled couples overcome their fears by leveraging a much greater _____.

> *The fear of the Lord is the beginning of wisdom; all who follow his precepts have good understanding.*
> —Psalm 111:10

> *When I am afraid, I put my trust in you.*
> —Psalm 56:3

Conclusion:

It's so much easier to maintain our pace and finish the marathon our marriage must run when we keep our core muscles of faith, integrity, poise, disciplines, endurance, and courage in good shape.

Read:

For a look at how to build these same character muscles into your kids, check out *Raising Kids Who Turn Out Right*.

Making This Yours

How did it go with implementing a practical application from the previous session? Share your successes and failures, because we learn from both.

What was one insight, principle, or illustration that stuck with you as you did your reading this week in *Grace Filled Marriage*?

Getting It Started

1. God tells us over and over again in his Word, *Do not be afraid.* How would owning that counsel change your day-to-day life? Can you tell of a time when you exercised your muscle of faith (trusted God) and God honored it?

2. Every day in our lives we're faced with big and small opportunities to do the right thing. Share about an incident when exercising your muscle of integrity was hard but paid off in the end. How about an example of doing the right thing— but the hard thing—in your marriage?

3. What are a few of your strengths (calling, convictions, capabilities) that could be maximized by flexing your muscle of discipline? How might this make you a better spouse? What are some grace-filled ways you could help your spouse maximize their strengths?

Taking It Deeper

1. These verses in Ecclesiastes may be new to you and a bit surprising:

> *Do not be overrighteous, neither be overwise–why destroy yourself? Do not be overwicked, and do not be a fool–why die before your time? It is good to grasp the one and not let go of the other. Whoever fears God will avoid all extremes.*
> —Ecclesiastes 7:16-18

Have there been seasons of extremes in your life? What was the impact of these out-of-balance choices in your own life and in the lives of others? What did you learn or are you still learning about keeping the bubble in the middle?

2. Whether we grew up in a home where our parents' marriage fell apart or we went through a divorce ourselves, we all have the opportunity to make our current marriage an example and encouragement of endurance to others.

   These verses remind us that having the same mind toward others as Christ has toward us can bring glory to God.

> *May the God who gives endurance and encouragement give you the same attitude of mind toward each other that Christ had, so that with one mind and one voice you may glorify the God and Father of our Lord Jesus Christ.*
> —Romans 15:5-6

How can enduring in your marriage bring glory to God and affect:

- your children,

- your friends,

- and our culture?

Bringing It Home

1. Using the metaphor of a marathon to describe marriage, how can we do better at managing our physical, mental, emotional, and spiritual lives to run the race before us and finish well?

2. What are you going through right now that could use the muscle of courage to help you have victory? It might be a rebellious child, an ex-spouse, illness, job stress, or challenges in your own marriage. Can you think of a few practical ways that Christ-like courage will help you stand firm in your faith?

When I am afraid, I put my trust in you.
—Psalm 56:3

3. How has this session challenged and/or confirmed your perceptions and assumptions about grace and/or marriage?

   Pre-Married Couples – How does this session apply to what you are dealing with in your countdown to marriage?

   Blended Couples – Share how this session applies to some of the unique complexities of blending two families.

Write it Down

As you commit to more grace in your own life and marriage, name one thing you learned in this session that you're going to put into practice this week. (Write this down before you dismiss.)

_____

_____

_____

_____

_____

_____

_____

Take a moment to turn to your spouse or fiancé and share what you just wrote down. Commit to encouraging each other this week.

This is a time for you to pray as a couple. Use the prayer below to guide you. Go ahead and pray even if you're by yourself.

Prayer

Father, give me faith to believe the promises of your Word, integrity to always do the right thing, poise to carry out the instructions in Scripture, discipline to harness my selfish nature, endurance to finish the race set before me, and courage to do them all with grace. Amen.

Prayer Requests:

_____

_____

_____

_____

_____

Read:

Please read chapter 10 in the book *Grace Filled Marriage* in order to get the most out of the upcoming session.

Engage...

...by signing up for the Family Matters blog, newsletter, or social media. Comment regularly to let us know what you think.

bit.ly/fmsignup

Introduction:

Whether we like to admit it or not, what holds our highest affections and focus plays a huge role in whether or not we get to enjoy the kind of heart connection or experience the kind of eternal impact God intended us to enjoy.

Since it's not a case of if we're aiming our lives at something, but where we're aiming them, why not aim them at something bigger than ourselves—something that has a higher purpose than here and now, you and me.

I. **Our relationship as married couples is defined by something that ultimately determines the kind of love, _____ _____, and depth of intimacy we will experience as couples.**

 A. Some people are defined by _____ goals.

 1. They spend a lot of time focused on their family.

 2. They spend a lot of time focused on the needs of their fellow man.

 3. They spend a lot of time focused on great causes.

 B. Some people are defined by _____ goals.

 1. They spend a lot of time focused on being obedient followers of God.

 2. They spend a lot of time focused on enhancing their eternal reward.

 C. Some people are defined by _____ goals.

 1. They spend a lot of time focused on the accumulation of _____.

    2. They spend a lot of time focused on the enhancement of their _____.

    3. They spend a lot of time focused on the exercise of _____.

    4. They spend a lot of time focused on the expansion of their _____.

II. **Since our relationship as married couples is going to have some target, it's vital that we _____ _____.**

    A. God's Word calls us to live _____ _____ lives.

> 'Love the Lord your God with all your heart and with all your soul and with all your strength and with all your mind'; and, 'Love your neighbor as yourself.'
> —Luke 10:27

    B. When we aim our marriage at true greatness, it gives our marriage deeper meaning and allows our marriage to make an eternal difference.

        1. True greatness is a passionate love for Jesus Christ that shows itself in an unquenchable love and concern for others.

        2. True marital greatness is our passionate love for Jesus Christ that shows itself in an unquenchable love and concern for each other.

    C. God's heart of grace is more likely to become the default mode of our marriage when the driving force behind it is not _____ love for God but rather _____ love for us.

> For Christ's love compels us… And he died for all, that those who live should no longer live for themselves but for him who died for them and was raised again.
>
> So from now on we regard no one from a worldly point of view… Therefore, if anyone is in Christ, the new creation has come: The old has gone, the new is here! All this is from God, who reconciled us to himself through Christ and gave us the ministry of reconciliation.
>
> —2 Corinthians 5:14-18

D. There are four wonderful qualities of true greatness that are direct extensions of God's gracious heart.

1. A _____ heart—not thinking less of yourself, but thinking of yourself less.

2. A _____ heart—an appreciation for what you have and for who has given it to you.

3. A _____ heart—a great delight in sharing with your spouse all that God has entrusted to you.

4. A _____ heart—an attitude describing the sacrificial assistance you enthusiastically make available to your spouse's needs and best interests regardless of the cost.

Conclusion:

* We start our marriage with love, but love by itself isn't enough to finish well. We need grace.

* Our marriage is meant to be a living illustration of the relationship Christ has with his bride, the Church. It's to be celebrated daily, enjoyed deeply, and used to transform us greatly. Only God's grace can accomplish any of these.

- A grace-filled marriage is determined not by the kind of relationship we have with each other, but by the kind of relationship we have with God.

- The key to loving each other in the power of God's grace is to love God first and love him most.

Making This Yours

How did it go with implementing a practical application from the previous session? Share your successes and failures, because we learn from both.

What was one insight, principle, or illustration that stuck with you as you did your reading this week in *Grace Filled Marriage*?

Getting It Started

1. Up until this point in your life, what have been your highest priorities? Be honest—there's no judgment here. To get you thinking, here are the goals we heard about in this session:

   Your family, the needs of your fellow man, great causes, being obedient followers of God, enhancing your eternal reward, accumulation of wealth, enhancement of beauty, exercise of power, expansion of fame.

2. We learned in this session that the litmus test for loving God is an authentic love for other people—a life focused upward and outward. How does this compare to our culture's prevailing view of marriage?

   How did your family of origin or your life before marriage either strengthen or undermine your ability to demonstrate a "truly great" love toward your spouse?

3. Tim reminds us that our love is limited but God's love is limitless. Why do you think Tim makes a distinction between God's love for us rather than our love for God being the driving force in a grace-filled marriage?

   What does this distinction assume about our relationship with God? How could this different driving force affect your daily interaction with your spouse? How could it affect the culture of grace in your home? (Think: application of the Napkin/House Model)

Taking It Deeper

1. Read this passage of Scripture in Luke.

> 'Love the Lord your God with all your heart and with all your soul and with all your strength and with all your mind'; and,
> 'Love your neighbor as yourself.'
> —Luke 10:27

In light of this Scripture, how can some of your previous goals remain part of your life and marriage but submit to the greater goals of loving God and loving others? Give some specific examples.

2. Read this passage of Scripture in 2 Corinthians.

> Christ's love compels us… And he died for all, that those who live should no longer live for themselves but for him who died for them and was raised again.
>
> So from now on we regard no one from a worldly point of view… Therefore, if anyone is in Christ, the new creation has come: The old has gone, the new is here! All this is from God, who reconciled us to himself through Christ and gave us the ministry of reconciliation.
>
> —2 Corinthians 5:14-19

Think of an instance in your marriage that required forgiveness and reconciliation. Apply the admonition in these verses to that scenario or to one you're going through right now.

Bringing It Home

1. What can the truly great qualities of humility, gratefulness, generosity, and a servant's heart do for some of the touchier issues of your marriage?

   For instance: money, your attitude toward your spouse's body, your in-laws, the way you treat your kids, your time, your attitude toward each other's hobbies, the tenderness you bring toward each other's burdens, the commitment you bring toward meeting each other's sexual needs?

Read:

For a look at how to aim your children at true greatness, check out the book and DVD study, *Raising Kids for True Greatness.*

---

2. Tim says that a grace-filled attitude is more likely to flourish within our marriage when we maintain heart connection to God through his Word, prayer, worship, and regular fellowship with mature, grace-filled believers. How have you found this to be true? Based on these four pillars of spiritual growth, what do you need to do to improve your heart connection to God?

3. How has this session challenged and/or confirmed your perceptions and assumptions about grace and/or marriage?

   Pre-Married Couples – How does this session apply to what you are dealing with in your countdown to marriage?

   Blended Couples – Share how this session applies to some of the unique complexities of blending two families.

Write it Down

As you commit to more grace in your own life and marriage, name one thing you learned in this session that you're going to put into practice this week. (Write this down before you dismiss.)

_____

_____

_____

_____

_____

_____

_____

Take a moment to turn to your spouse or fiancé and share what you just wrote down. Commit to encouraging each other this week.

This is a time for you to pray as a couple. Use the prayer below to guide you. Go ahead and pray even if you're by yourself.

Prayer

Lord, thank you so much for this study on grace and marriage and thank you for the grace you show me when I don't deserve it. Help me to let your love and grace flow through me to my spouse as I endeavor to meet their inner needs, set their heart free, build their character muscles, and aim with them at a life of true greatness. I ask all these things in the name of the great lover of my soul, Jesus. Amen.

Prayer Requests:

_____

_____

_____

_____

_____

_____

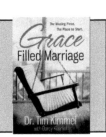

Read:

We encourage you to read the epilogue, Good to Grace, in the book *Grace Filled Marriage* as you tie a bow on this study. (One of you could read it out loud at the close of this session.)

Your study of *Grace Filled Marriage* is a beginning for understanding how God's grace can make all the difference in your own marriage. You're just getting started and we want to encourage you to continue as you learn more about grace-based relationships. Please read the "*Where to go from here*" section, starting on the next page for some tips and guidelines for how to keep pursuing grace-based relationships.

Pray...

...for your spouse for the next month by subscribing to our *31 Days of Prayer for Your Spouse* feature.

bit.ly/31forfamily

Where To Go from Here: A Guide for Going Deeper

Now that you have finished this foundational study on Grace Filled Marriage, it's important to ask yourself, "Where do I go from here?" Our follow-up resources complete the "big picture" and equip you to let grace-based relationships transform your family and your own life as well.

Encouragement and reinforcement are key ingredients to any new endeavor. Talking and praying through these concepts with others will help you develop the mind-set of a grace-filled spouse.

We encourage you to:

Do Another DVD Study

We have many more great video studies for you and your group, such as:

- *Grace Filled Marriage Part 2* (check **familymatters.net** for release date)
- *Grace Based Parenting Part 1: Creating an Atmosphere of Grace*
- *Grace Based Parenting Part 2: Building Character*
- *Grace Based Parenting Part 3: Aiming your Child at True Greatness*
- *Hurried Family: Help for the Hurried Home*
- *Extreme Grandparenting: The Ride of Your Life*

A complete list can be found on the resource pages of this workbook or at our website, **familymatters.net**.

Read a Book

Each book has its own small group study guide in the back which equips parents and couples to make these principles a lifestyle, helps them remember what they just learned, and provides real-life examples of how to apply these ideas to daily life.

Lead a Study

Why not take it a step further and start your own group? Maybe you could do this in your neighborhood, school, or church. One of the best ways to learn something well is to teach it to others. We have fantastic facilitator support material on our website for all those who step out to lead one of these transformational studies.

Attend a Conference

For an exciting and equipping experience, come to one of our fun, fast-paced events. Go to **familymatters.net** to see where we are holding one of our next life-changing marriage or parenting conferences.

Host a Conference

Bring a Family Matters' marriage or parenting conference to your church and community. Let us tell you about the incredible possibilities available for hearing the grace-based message. Find out more at **familymatters.net/events**.

Stay Connected

Our web community is there for you as you live out your marriage and raise your family with grace-based relationships. Go to **familymatters.net** and take advantage of all of the helpful family tools.

- **familymatters.net** (a treasure trove of help and hope for your family)
- Family Matters Minute (grace-based nuggets of wisdom for your parenting journey)
- Family Matters' Blog, Facebook, and Twitter
- Family Matters' App (available through the Apple App Store or Google Play)

www.familymatters.net

How to Become a Friend of God by Accepting His Grace

The big picture of grace-based relationships is built on a foundation of faith in Jesus Christ. If you've never entered into a personal relationship with Christ, there's not a better time than now. Below, you will find all you need to lay that foundation of faith.

God Loves Us

> *"For God so loved the world that he gave his one and only Son,*
> *that whoever believes in him shall not perish*
> *but have eternal life."*
> —John 3:16

We matter to God. he made us and he wants to have a relationship with us.

We are Sinful and Separated from God

> *For all have sinned and fall short of the glory of God.*
> —Romans 3:23

But we've rebelled against God. Whether actively or passively, we've all disobeyed him. And our sins have separated us from him and broken off the relationship.

The Ultimate Consequence of Sin is Death

> *For the wages of sin is death …*
> —Romans 6:23(a)

Besides causing separation from God, the sins we have committed must be punished, and the penalty we owe is death. This means physical death as well as spiritual death — eternal separation from God for eternity in a place called hell.

Jesus is the Only Way to God

For Christ died for sins once for all … to bring you to God.
—1 Peter 3:18

The good news is God loves us so much that he provided a bridge over which we can find forgiveness, restore our relationship, and spend eternity with him in heaven. he built it by coming to earth as one of us and dying on the cross to pay the death penalty we owed. But it's not enough to know about this or even agree with it…

We Need to Receive Christ Personally

…to all who received him, to those who believed in his name, he gave the right to become children of God.
—John 1:12

God has provided this bridge back to him, but we need to respond to him by crossing to the other side. We do this by humbly admitting to God that we have rebelled against him, and we need his forgiveness and leadership. This simple act of trust and obedience results in our being pardoned and our debt being paid. By faith through prayer, you can receive Christ right now. If the following prayer expresses your desire, pray it now.

The Prayer of Restoration

Dear Jesus, I know that I need you. Thank you for dying on the cross and paying the price for my sins. I admit that I have fallen short of your standards and ask you to forgive me. Thank you for your forgiveness. Please become the leader of my life and shape me into the person you want me to be. Amen.

The Bible says that the angels rejoice when someone accepts Christ as their Savior (Luke 15:10). Make sure you tell someone your good news!

Resources in this section are available from **shop.familymatters.net**.

Books

Grace Based Parenting

This book is a must for parents who want to love their kids the way God loves his. With humor and pathos, it goes into depth on how to meet our children's inner heart needs and grant the four freedoms that can make an atmosphere of grace a permanent condition in your home.

Raising Kids Who Turn Out Right

With warmth and conviction, Dr. Tim Kimmel outlines a plan for building your child from the inside out by transferring character — faith, integrity, poise, disciplines, endurance and courage— into their heart.

Raising Kids for True Greatness

Wouldn't it be great to have kids who are humble, grateful, generous and have a servant's heart? Dr. Tim Kimmel shows you how to turn greatness into the DNA of your own life so you can pass it on to your children. This book also helps you prepare your child to answer the three biggest questions of life and is filled with many "Top Ten" lists for applying the principles of true greatness in everyday life.

Little House on the Freeway

Don't let busyness and the temptation to "keep up with the Joneses" rob you of the peace and incredible quality of relationships God created for you. This book will equip you and your family with confidence and practical, stress-saving skills as you take the off-ramp to sanity, peace, and family harmony.

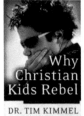

Why Christian Kids Rebel

This book provides help and hope for parents dealing with a rebellious teen and teaches them how to lead that child back into a walk of faith. This book also offers a doable plan for parents of young children who want to avoid having them walk away from God in a few short years.

50 Ways to Really Love Your Kids

Because we love our kids – really love them – we're always on the lookout for new ways to make their precious lives even better. That's where this little book can make a big difference. Here are fifty practical ways that can sharpen your ability to deliver that love into the very core of their hearts.

Homegrown Heroes

Of all the values and skills we need to build into our children's hearts, courage tops the list. Courage is what will motivate our children to do what they ought to do in any given situation. This sweetly powerful book will turn your good intentions into a plan that works to give your children their best shot at a great and meaningful life.

High Cost of High Control

No one likes to be controlled, including your spouse and kids. Life can be a whole lot more pleasant around your house when you determine to keep your kids under control, rather than try to control them. Dr. Tim Kimmel gives you the biblical strategy for breaking free from the pain of controlling people and how to avoid being a high-controller yourself.

Basic Training for a Few Good Men

Dads, your child is looking to you to lead the way into the battlefield of life. You'll learn how to be the kind of man who flourishes at his work, draws the best out of his wife, makes it easy for his kids to look up to him, and finds joy serving in God's army – all delivered with wit and punch as you eagerly turn each page.

Extreme Grandparenting: The Ride of Your Life

Are you ready to take grandparenting to the next level? You'll learn how to make the most of this significant opportunity to imprint the next generation with grace. Discover how you can be not only a mentor but a spiritual rock for your grandchildren. This book is full of fresh new ideas to connect to the heart of your grandchildren.

In Praise of Plan B

Life doesn't always go according to plan — your plan that is. These twenty lighthearted, encouraging stories will remind you that making the most of whatever happens is a much better way to go through life. You'll laugh until you cry and cry until you need to laugh as you look at life as it can be when you step aside and let God call the shots.

Connecting Church and Home: A Grace Based Partnership

We are faced with a culture of busy churches and overwhelmed families that need a clear plan to pass a spiritual legacy to the hearts of their kids. Tim Kimmel shows how churches and parents can work together in a grace-based partnership to make each other's efforts more impactful. Church ministry leaders will find a complete plan that can be tailored to any size church. Parents will find a

simple path that will empower them to exercise their spiritual influence. Both will discover the power of grace by leveraging the influence of church and home.

Grace Filled Marriage: The Missing Piece, The Place to Start

You start your love story with dreams and end it with memories. But if you invite Jesus along for the ride and let his grace weave its way through all those memories, you'll get to finish your story well. God's grace will prove to be sufficient all the way to the end. Whether you have a good marriage or one in serious need of help, you simply cannot do it in your own power. To have a marriage that thrives, you need grace. Grace Filled Marriage explores the daily reality of a life lived out with a commitment to treating our spouse the way God treats us—with grace. In this provocative look at love, we'll see how God's grace plays out in our marriage as we navigate through the areas of sex, kids, conflict, aging, and endings…gracefully.

Kids Flag Page

Consider this the operating manual that should have come with each of your kids — but didn't. This colorful and engaging game is a fun way for parents to interact with their kids and truly discover the heart of each child — who God created them to be. It also comes with an eye-opening book that thoroughly outlines a strategy for each of your children, including those strong-willed ones in your home.

Video Studies

The Grace Based Parenting Video Series

Part 1: Creating an Atmosphere of Grace

This is a fun, refreshing small group study that gives parents a realistic job description for raising spiritually strong children who grow up with a sense of calm and a heart full of purpose. As you watch the DVD and use the helpful discussion guide, you will learn to meet your children's inner heart needs and grant the four freedoms that can make an atmosphere of grace a permanent condition in your home.

Part 2: Building Character

This exciting study is a practical strategy for raising kids who turn out right by instilling character into their hearts. These seven powerful sessions, with helpful discussion guides and leaders' tools, will show you how to model and teach your children about faith, integrity, poise, disciplines, endurance, and courage.

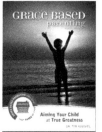

Part 3: Aiming at True Greatness

This eye-opening study exposes our culture's definition of success (wealth, beauty, power and fame) as a goal unworthy of our pursuit. Instead, it describes the spiritual adventure we can live when we aim our children at a higher goal – True Greatness. The DVD and discussion guide present four characteristics of truly great people along with many other helpful insights designed to equip your children to answer life's three biggest questions. The study also equips parents to help their children answer the three most important questions in life.

The Hurried Family Video Study

In this age of stress and crazy schedules, you can never have enough help and hope amidst the hurry. This small group study will empower you and your family with confidence and practical, stress-saving skills as you take the off-ramp to sanity, peace and family harmony. Includes powerful discussion guide and leaders' tools.

Extreme Grandparenting: The Ride of Your Life.

As a grandparent, you have a valuable opportunity to influence and connect to the heart of your grandchildren. Make the most of it by gathering a group of like-minded grandparents and going through this interactive study together. You'll receive practical teaching and enjoy lively discussions as you learn how to play a key role in the generation that you will one day leave in charge.

Basic Training for a Few Good Men.

This push and play study couldn't be easier for men's groups and retreats. Complete with discussion guides and leaders' tools, this exciting study gives husbands and dads marching orders for moral and spiritual leadership in the key areas of family, work, community and church – all delivered powerfully, with warmth and humor.

Grace Filled Marriage: The Missing Piece. The Place to Start.
Part 1 and Part 2 (check **gracefilledmarriage.net** for Part 2 release date).

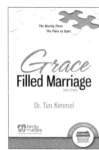

Just about every married couple starts out with a lot of love in their hearts for each other. But real-time life and the personal issues we all bring to the arrangement put that love to quite a test. This often puts wear and tear on their friendship, their roles as parents, and steals a lot of joy and passion from their sexual relationship. Love does a great job of getting us married, but it's God's grace that can keep us married. We all need to wrap grace around our love to keep it fresh and ensure that it grows stronger with time. This video study is a love-altering journey based on Tim and Darcy's game-changing book, Grace Filled Marriage.

About Family Matters

> **The Vision of Family Matters**
> is to see families transformed by God's grace into
> instruments of reformation and restoration.

Family Matters educates, encourages, and equips families to:

- live relevant, joyful, and victorious lives.
- bring the best out of each other in their daily relationships.
- pass a legacy of God's grace from one generation to the next.

Family Matters offers families help and hope for every age and stage of life through our:

- Conferences and keynote events
- Best-selling books
- Practical, well-researched video studies
- Interactive and transformational family tools

You Can Be a Part of Building Strong Families

Family Matters is a non-profit, charitable organization committed to strengthening the vital relationships within families. It is a member of the Evangelical Council for Financial Accountability.

The faithful donations of people who share a kindred heart for strong Christian homes enables Family Matters to create new ways and means to bring health and strength to today's families.

If you would like to get more information on how to make Family Matters part of your charitable giving portfolio, please call 1-800-467-4596 or go online to **www.familymatters.net**.

Building grace-based relationships is what Family Matters is all about.

Fill-in-the-Blank Answer Guide

Session 1:

heart
adjustments
performance
setbacks
priorities
selfishness
least expressed
nice
deeply need

Session 2:

Me
Love If
Pious
blocks
Gospel
transform
grace

Session 3:

big-picture
graciously
full
secure love
accept
affiliation
affection

Session 4:

obligation
manipulate
punish
demand
defraud
bless
enthusiasm
desire
delight

Session 5:

significant
affirm
attention
admonish
strong hope
abilities
accomplishments
adventure

Session 6:

different
moral
vulnerable
safe
candid
mistakes
destroy
holy mercy
temper

Session 7:

faith
trust
obey
integrity
protection
poise
extremes
balance
disciplines
potential
endurance
courage
fear

Session 8:

life impact
noble
holy
success
wealth
beauty
power
fame
aim high
truly great
our
his
humble
grateful
generous
servant's

Tim and Darcy Kimmel have been married longer than most people doing this study have been alive. That doesn't make them experts; just veterans.

They didn't get far into living out their love story before they realized that they'd need a whole lot more than their on-board affection for each other to see it go the distance. Between the competition they were getting from the culture that surrounded them and their internal bent towards self-centered interests, it was obvious that their relationship was destined for mediocrity, disappointment, or even worse unless something radically changed.

That's where God's grace came to the rescue. God is always giving us something we desperately need, but don't necessarily deserve. It's when they decided to get serious about treating each other the way Jesus treats them that their friendship, their focus, the way they treated each other as lovers, and the way they teamed as parents gave them something to consistently smile about.

The missing ingredient in most marriages isn't love; it's grace. Love does a great job of getting us married, but it's God's grace that can keep us married. We all need to wrap grace around our love to keep it fresh and insure that it grows stronger with time.

The Grace Filled Marriage Video Study is a love-altering journey based on Tim and Darcy's game-changing book, *Grace Filled Marriage*. You're going to LOVE this study!

Family Matters has been helping raise the spiritual, emotional, and relational stock value of families for well over three decades. Its goal is to see families transformed by the power of God's grace into instruments of reformation and restoration. When the vital relationships within families are guided by God's truth, while at the same time tempered by His grace—everyone in the family picture wins.

Over the years Family Matters has shown millions of people how to make God's grace the defining feature of their homes. To learn more about their life changing conferences, books and family tools, please visit us at www.familymatters.net.

building grace-based relationships

View Other Family
Matters Resources:
bit.ly/shopfamilymatters

The History of
Family Matters:
bit.ly/historyfm